# Stars and Sparrows Alike

*poems by*

# Ryan Apple

*Finishing Line Press*
Georgetown, Kentucky

# Stars and Sparrows Alike

Copyright © 2020 by Ryan Apple
ISBN 978-1-64662-353-2 First Edition
All rights reserved under International and Pan-American Copyright Conventions. No part of this book may be reproduced in any manner whatsoever without written permission from the publisher, except in the case of brief quotations embodied in critical articles and reviews.

## ACKNOWLEDGMENTS

I am grateful to the following journals and anthologies in which some of the poems of this book first appeared:

*A Hundred Gourds*: "EXOPLANET FOUND"
*Adam, Eve, and the Riders of the Apocalypse*: "Wandering Stars"
*Chaparral Poetry Forum*: "Portrait of a Friend's Daughter, Senior Year"
*Ice Pop Poetry*: "Arena Rock Anthems for Easy Piano" and "Embryonic"
*In a Strange Land: Introducing Ten Kingdom Poets*: "Opportunity", "Polar Vortex 2019", and "The Atomic Weight of Glory"
*Orchard Poetry Journal*: "Sonnet"
*Peninsula Poets*: "Sundown"
*Portage Magazine*: "Removing an Old Acquaintance From My List of Contacts"
*Time of Singing*: "ember glow" and "well spoken words"

Thank you to the many friends, family members, and fellow poets who have directly and indirectly supported my work.

Special thanks are due to Darcie, Dorian, Elliana, Micah, Annissa, Selah, and Asher, and to the Delta Community Christian Church family. Together, we are God's poem.


Publisher: Leah Huete de Maines
Editor: Christen Kincaid
Cover Art: Darcie Apple, www.pixabay.com
Author Photo: Darcie Apple
Cover Design: Elizabeth Maines McCleavy

Order online: www.finishinglinepress.com
also available on amazon.com

Author inquiries and mail orders:
Finishing Line Press
P. O. Box 1626
Georgetown, Kentucky 40324
U. S. A.

# Table of Contents

*I. Sparrows*

Portrait of a Friend's Daughter, Senior Year................1
Perspective................2
Removing an Old Aquaintance From My List of Contacts................3
Arena Rock Anthems for Easy Piano................4
Embryonic................5
Last Nights in Jericho................6
Sundown................7

*II. Like*

Disappearing People................11
April 11................12
Sonnet................13
Letter to My Son................14

*III. Stars*

Polar Vortex 2019................17
The Atomic Weight of Glory................18
Opportunity................20
An Angel Considers Taking a Lunch Break................22
Wandering Stars................23
Ode to My Mbira................24
The Age of Accountability................26

## I. Sparrows

        ember glow
        in the homeless camp
        winter stars

## Portrait of a Friend's Daughter, Senior Year

A warm September night, she tests her legs
on the trampoline. The air is humid, the grass
deep green and damp. Her springing

tells the tempo and time to all the songs of night:
the chorus of distant traffic, the buzz of insects
burrowed in trees, and the trill of the mockingbird stretching

its adolescent wings. But lately, she's been soaking in
the music of the spheres, the silence

planets and stars have sung from time only God can tell—
the profound and secret harmony she hears
alone. Her sister is already sleeping, her mother
busy in the kitchen. As for her father and me in the sunroom,

we have grown deaf to their song. The whole wide universe
is waking now around her, the starlight calling her higher;
bound by bound, she is breaking the spell of gravity.

## Perspective

If I come to spend my last days here as well,
wheeled out of my room by an aid
to watch volunteers wheedle holiday tunes
from the dining hall's upright piano,

then may I overlook my helper's indifference
and that of the workers forgoing the games,
denying themselves the sweet satisfaction
of lining blue chips on a cardboard square.

May I still call it generational difference
which really, I'd say then, is all about subtlety.
See the youth like their everything fast and loud
and new, always new—young people tire so quickly.

It takes a mature mind to appreciate slowness,
to solve the hundred piece puzzle,
to measure out words like peas on a spoon,
to track the goldfish as it circuits the bowl.

# Removing An Old Acquaintance From My List of Contacts

I am deleting your phone number today,
erasing your email, and dragging your name
right into the trash.

Small wonder we call techies unsocial.
You'd think I was wielding a voodoo doll,
each numeric digit a finger or toe,
backspacing all trace of you from existence.

Perhaps semantics could help.
Let's reframe this in terms of release: Today
I let go my end of the wire,
to send it racing a thousand miles
through cities and rivers, forests and farms.
And when the slack finally snaps on your side,
may your stride be lightened wherever your road lies.

May your mind no longer have to stutter step around
me when you hear Bach on guitar
or see the word "Apple" with a capital A.

Let's face it Paul, and be honest
as only strangers can,
this day to de-clutter was bound to come,
tossing aside knick-knacks of our past,
your name a hurdle to dialing a friend,
my fading image a smudge on the glass
somewhere overlooking your faraway world.

**Arena Rock Anthems For Easy Piano**

Here you will find the most iconic anthems of a generation, now carefully arranged for the beginning pianist. Finally you can relive the exhilarating sounds of Boston, Def Leppard, Queen, and many more, all from the comfort of home.

What sets these songs apart is their raw power; power to bring you indelibly back to that rush of euphoria you knew was more than a feeling. True, that power has distilled in the journey from stadium to bar to elevator down to the fine music retailer you are shopping today—but no more so than the sparks of those magnetic gods of rock 'n roll have disseminated into the hearts of their devoted fans.

So consider your difficult role as performer. This is your electric past, conjured up in an autocrat present. And that past self is a foreigner here, often misappropriated with malignant intention.

The tension is real. It's there when the wild-haired teens steer by and you stroke your invisible mullet. These melodies and lyrics still charged with hysteria, such a magical mysteria, and you can't stop this feeling. You can't stop this lighter flame fire.

**Embryonic**

Our secret so young
we sign it all evening

around the table
across the room

a lift in your eyelids
or turn of my lip
this language coded
as our DNA

                fusing
inside of your body

too soon will begin
the task of translation
Let them stay unaware
and your eyes be my oceans

(I could swim your deep green
oceans teeming with life)

Let my hand tether yours
steer us safe to the kitchen
where harbored we'll whisper
of crossings ahead

and name the new worlds
just edging our sights

## Last Nights in Jericho
*Joshua 2*

Between customers
she stands at the window,
scanning outside the fortified wall.
    *Impenetrable*
*to all but the gods.*

The spies, she knows,
are long past the vineyards,
surely beyond the honeycomb hills.
    *Yahweh's army*
*coming for her.*

She fingers the cord,
holds it close to her heart,
scarlet and tattered,
    *but the origin*
*delicate cotton…*

*blossoms pure as milk,*
*whiter than snow.*

**Sundown**
> *Ephesians 4:26*

In pre-marriage counseling they told us to never
let the sun go down on our anger.
Whimsy notwithstanding,

the warning seemed quaint
since electricity has deemed our clocks
the arbiters of time,

and sailors now watch weather.com,
having jettisoned their nursery rhymes
about red skies.

But in the wake of our disagreement,
with the sky so overcast
(I circled the same point;

turning, you drifted off),
I just stared into the clouded night, wondering
how we might navigate to common ground.

**II. Like**

                    well spoken words
                    listen how a rivulet
                    carries the ocean

**Disappearing People**
    *For Dorian, on her 12th birthday*

Remember when you were five?
I was the great magician
who made coins, blocks and toys disappear.

You were my devoted audience,
demanding for the encore
"Daddy, disappear me!"

Could I transport you to another dimension?
Or at the count of three, could I dematerialize you,
expertly spacing your atoms throughout our living room;
all those vocal cords vibrating in silent laughter?

Would you trust me to reappear you in the right order?
Daddy, who doesn't know a neutron from a neuron?
Or could I hide you up my sleeve?
And do so without letting you in on the illusion?

I don't need to explain to you
that these are rhetorical questions.
Neither do I need to tell you
that we both age,
and I am losing power so quickly.

But truly I tell you,
daughter of mine,
truly I say:
before you thought I could walk on water
we were visited by a man who did,
the man whose stories I have told you again and again,

in fact,
even now I am remembering the time when he disappeared from
Emmaus
and reappeared in a locked room some seven miles away and
how he asked the audience for a piece of fish
and ate it before their wondering eyes.

## April 11

My sweet Selah
I will not forget this day
your mother poured you out
all four pounds seven ounces
Skin to skin I savored
the fragrance of your hair

This was Holy Week
maybe the day the woman
emptied her pint of perfume
anointing Jesus' head

or maybe the day
                      he hung on the cross
and hanging off his crown of thorns
spikenard scented icicles
of blood and sweat fell down

I never had time
to tell you these stories
How some had whispered What a waste
Such a waste some said that day
Why this extravagance?

Honestly Selah one time I asked
the same indignant question
but I do know better now

Forgive me Selah
I loved you much but
did not recognize
this day was my anointing

**Sonnet**

O Christ, when you return to bring your reign
Will sleeping infants hear your trumpet call?
Are they invited to your banquet hall
Which welcomes in the poor, the blind, and lame?

Think of non-sentient stars, summoned by name—
These ancient lights like common sparrows fall.
You track our graying hairs; you count them all
And weigh an hour and century the same.

If you recall the smallest vein you knit
And stitch the robes the least of these will wear;
If you do not call nascent lungs unfit
But find within the faintest cries a prayer,
Then wake our daughter; dry a mother's tears,
And hundredfold redeem the stolen years.

**Letter to My Son**
 *A long time after our landowner's return*

Come meet me in my vineyard,
or if you like, your orchard,
in the fig tree's shade.

Either way, we'll reminisce
the inch-time of the caterpillar,
and the minute of the mustard seed.

Tell me again of that instant
when yeast was stirring in the dough,
firstfruits ripening on the vine
and the rock rising into mountain
right beneath our feet.

See it's not that I would have us go back—
not to those seconds clouds obscured the sun,
that hour before the guns and knives
were forged into our garden tools or
left to rust away.

But recalling the ancient stories with you
is like glimpsing the mist of a dream
shimmering in the break of day.
So wonderfully hard to believe there was
that embryonic moment, that time
before you called me brother,
that fleeting age I called you son.

## III. Stars

*EXOPLANET FOUND*
reading outside the café
i feel a raindrop

## Polar Vortex 2019

There's a primal kind of clarity
when the whole city closes down
and you survey from the driveway
your arctic neighborhood
a collage of distant latitudes

There's a heightened sensitivity
in wind chill 40 below
when the ghostly wisps
entwine your feet
when you feel them scratch your heels

when overhead this silent land
you overhear a high-pitched ring
like shearing through sheet metal skies

and high above this desert snow
you sense the arcing flight
of some albino creature
shrieking through the polar air

Just days ago
you disbelieved the augury of weather seers
their urgency to track this one
its swooping here and there

Now the sages pound the drums
deep within your blood rushed ears
Keep vigilance out there
they warn Watch
you don't let it bite

## The Atomic Weight of Glory

Before thumbing through that office magazine,
waiting to have a tooth filled,
you had never imagined yourself to be
such a walking chemistry kit.

Who knew manganese's tiny vial
held a skeleton key to your sundry moods?
Or that smuggled within your bloodstream
was a penny's worth of liquid gold?

So here you are: 34 pounds carbon,
4 pounds nitrogen,
then topped off with traces of tungsten,
caesium, chromium, arsenic—

till finally: *Just add water.*
And there accounts well more
than 99.9%—
plenty good enough. At least for some,

                                      though not for you

ever since that breakfast on the canyon floor.
You hadn't even known you were hungry
till lightning flashed in a clear blue sky
revealing the frost to be wafers of bread.

And then, rushing down the cold ravine,
a strange wind filled your lungs,
tungsten formed a filament,
and your whole being shot

with light. You felt magnesium and phosphorus ignite
and burn within your bones,
fueled by a secret element
unperceived in the whole of the world.

Lighter than lithium,
more precious than gold,
and assurance of when—
yes, one fine day—

at last you will finally be whole.

**Opportunity**

One time he took the devil's hand,
weary and famished, needing help
to finish the final ascent—
                                but oh what a view.

The Mediterranean blue,
ships of Sidon, Lebanon cedars
sparrows and screech owls
hillsides with thousands of sheep

Galileans casting nets
women at the well
blind men begging poolside
Herod's temple
the temple of Artemis

Pharaoh's magicians
Celtic druids
Brahmans and Sudra
pigs and pygmies
roving wolves, hungry lions
fattened calves, skittish sheep
                                how many million sheep?
sheep without a shepherd


The long way back was less picturesque.
Lonely rocks like loaves of bread
Mirages masking burning sand
(what of the promised desert streams?)

Illusions of Nazareth
Jerusalem
and then even Rome, how it could have
right then all been his


And who among his hearers would know
it was no hyperbole whenever he posed:
                    what good is the world in hand when
the seller demands your soul?

## An Angel Considers Taking a Lunch Break
*Genesis 3-9*

For two thousand years I have kept my guard,
and most of the mortals have kept their distance.
But I have wrestled men. I have
resisted women.

I remember the children shielding their eyes,
stumbling up to touch my glittering robe—
a little annoying at the time,
the flaming sword juggled high out of reach
as I nudged them off to find another
garden to play in.

*** 

Sometimes when the ghosts
of screams drift in from the east, I wonder
what reaches from here to there.
If the wind turned just right, and if this fragrance
whistled through the thickets, could it find someone
sensing paradise.  And when that someone came,
would I run them off so quickly.

Or would I hack through all the thorns and thistles
and stomp over fungus
and fallen branches until I could point and say
There! Just
look how it still blossoms! Arching, proffering
all that burgundy,
succulent—

No (if you're wondering),
no I've never tasted their fruit.
But someone should.
                        So heavy it hangs there,
ripe as raindrops dangling from the sky
as if awaiting some summons to all
come crashing down at once.

## Wandering Stars
*after Jude*

You will hardly notice it happening at first
so watch for the signs
of leaving your place assigned in the heavens.

Autumn will grow longer.
Your oceans will crash more closely to shore.
You will note more cloudy days, but experience less rain.

When you see these things taking place,
know for certain your star is following its instinct,
searching for secret dimensions draped in the fabric of space.

How large it will seem in your sky;
how brightly it will sparkle!—
and how strongly it will pull you to follow.

Instinct, you know, draws a moth to the flame.
But here there is no flame. Only a black hole.

**Ode to My Mbira**

When you arrived last October
as newest sibling to piano, guitar,
and little ukulele, before I

could even pronounce your name, you
captured me with that buzzing rasp
coating your bell-like voice. I

wondered over strangely arranged
secondhand metal keys, how
this wandering path came to be
the way you traverse a three-octave span. You

do not share our accent, our
all white key Ionian scale; your
temperament wild and uneven.
                                            (Once, I

showed you off to someone who said
you would sound much prettier
if we clipped off your bottle cap rattlers.)

***

Humble body of wood and wire,
song through radio static,
wind chime in the rain,
marimba on the ocean surf,

how can I speak of you if not by way of myself?
I know so little of your own tradition,
your polyrhythmic complexity,
your circular meditations of melody.

But just to hear your simplest words,
say when you ring a low perfect fifth,
it's as if all the colorful sounds of the world
come down to this one ancient resonance,

the tones from which all music was born,
the divine serenade to palette of earth
calling forth  *Let there be.*

## The Age of Accountability

Was it the great,
awful day of the Lord
when the cosmic calendar
skipped over summer
and my innocent spring turned
to fall?

Or the day you passed by
in the ripening garden
and saw I was ready for love?

Shall I call it the dull
milk-white moon eclipsed
in bloodguilt, ashen
in the glare of its heavenly lord?

Or rather my wakening
eyes to the sky,
alert to your covenant sign,
to the sevenfold beauty of light?

Not so much the lawful degree
when the tea kettle's importunate cry
signals of all that is slipping away,

but more the approach to the ocean,
and the pitch and degree
of waves to the shore.
Eternal the invitation,
the rhythmic rise and retreat
calling us into the depths.

**R**yan **Apple** lives in Lansing, Michigan, with his wife Darcie and their six children. Since 2006, he has been employed as a music professor at Great Lakes Christian College. An avid guitarist, he has recorded an album featuring works from the 1300s through the present day.

His poetry has been published or is forthcoming in a number of journals, including *Ekstasis, Peninsula Poets, Portage Magazine, Solum Journal,* and the Poiema Poetry Series anthologies *Adam, Eve, and the Riders of the Apocalypse* and *In a Strange Land: Introducing Ten Kingdom Poets.*

Ryan enjoys sharing life with his local church family, ping-pong, playing guitar and mbira, and video games with two or less buttons. Read more and listen to his music at www.ryanapple.net.

www.ingramcontent.com/pod-product-compliance
Lightning Source LLC
LaVergne TN
LVHW041517070426
835507LV00012B/1634